TWO-CHORD SONGS
FOR UKULELE

ISBN 978-1-4803-8241-1

HAL•LEONARD®
CORPORATION
7777 W. BLUEMOUND RD. P.O. BOX 13819 MILWAUKEE, WI 53213

Visit Hal Leonard Online at
www.halleonard.com

ABC

Words and Music by Alphonso Mizell, Frederick Perren,
Deke Richards and Berry Gordy

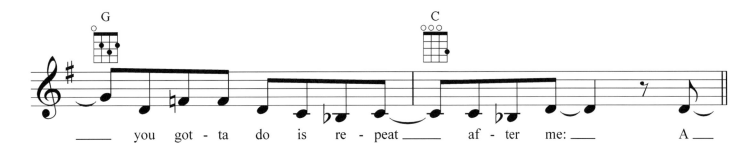

you got - ta do is re - peat ___ af - ter me: ___ A ___

Chorus

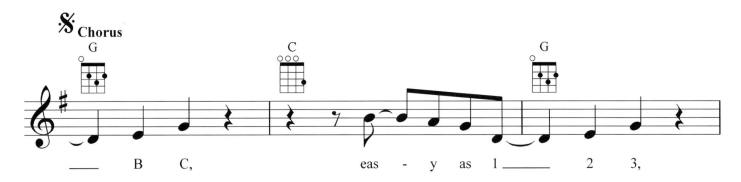

___ B C, eas - y as 1 ___ 2 3,

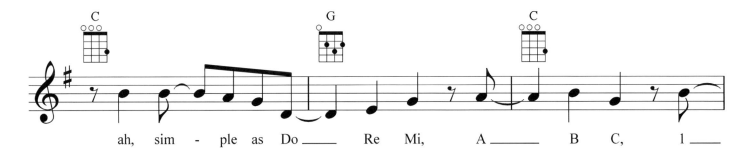

ah, sim - ple as Do ___ Re Mi, A ___ B C, 1 ___

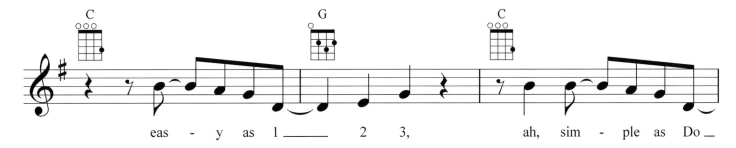

___ 2 3, ba - by, you and me, ___ girl. A B C,

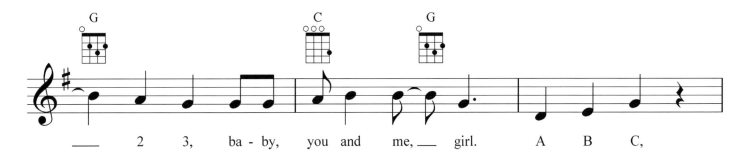

eas - y as 1 ___ 2 3, ah, sim - ple as Do ___

To Coda

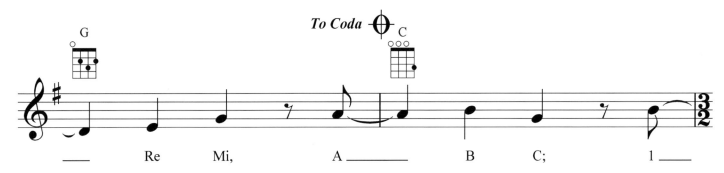

___ Re Mi, A ___ B C; 1 ___

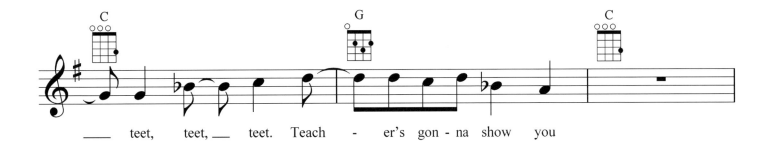

___ teet, teet, ___ teet. Teach - er's gon - na show you_

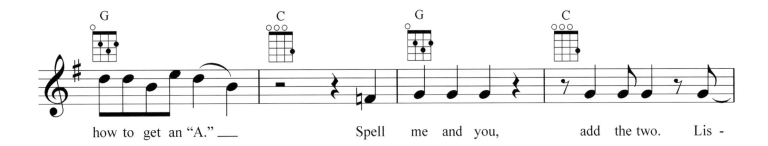

_how to get an "A." ___ Spell me and you, add the two. Lis -_

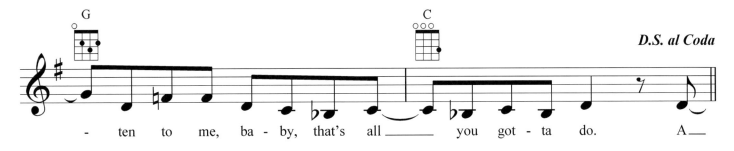

D.S. al Coda

_- ten to me, ba - by, that's all _____ you got - ta do. A ____

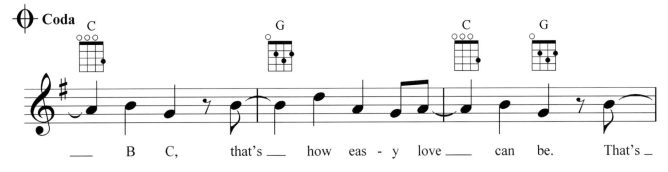

Coda

___ B C, that's ___ how eas - y love ____ can be. That's __

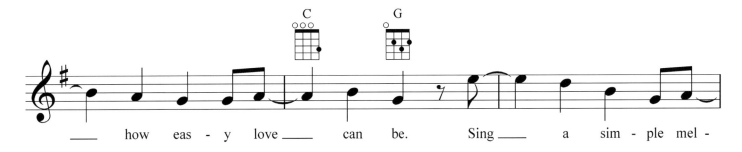

____ how eas - y love ____ can be. Sing ____ a sim - ple mel -_

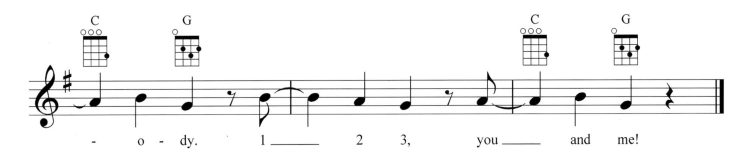

_- o - dy. 1 _____ 2 3, you ____ and me!_

Brick House

Words and Music by Lionel Richie, Ronald LaPread, Walter Orange, Milan Williams, Thomas McClary and William King

7

brick house. ___ Ow, that la-dy's stacked ___ and that's a fact, ___

ain't hold-in' noth-in' back. ___ Oh, she's a brick ___ house, ___ yeah. ___

She's the one, ___ the on-ly one, ___ built like an Am-a-zon. ___

Verse

2. The clothes she wear, ___ her sex-y ways ___ make an

old ___ man ___ wish for young-er days, ___ yeah, yeah.

She knows she's built and knows how to please. __

Sho' nuf can knock a strong __ man to his knees, __ 'cause she's a

Outro-Chorus

Am   Bm   Am   Bm   Am   Bm

brick house. __
Brick house. __

Yeah, __ she's might-y, might-y, __ just

Am   Bm   Am   Bm   Am   Bm

let-tin' it all __ hang out. __ Ah, she's a brick house. __

{ That
{ Yeah,

Am   Bm   Am   Bm   Am

la-dy's stacked __ and that's a fact, __ ain't hold-in' noth-in' back. __ Ow!
she's the one, __ the on-ly one, __ built like an Am-a-zon. __ Yeah!

Copperhead Road

Words and Music by Steve Earle

1. Well, my name's John Lee Pet-ti-more.
(2., 3.) *See additional lyrics*

Same as my dad-dy and his dad-dy be-fore. You hard-ly ev-er saw Grand-dad-dy down here. He on-ly come to town a-bout twice a year.

He'd buy a hun - dred pounds of yeast and some cop - per line.

Ev - 'ry - bod - y knew that he made moon - shine.

Now, the rev - e - nue man want - ed Grand - dad - dy bad. He head - ed up a hol - ler with ev - 'ry - thing he had. _ Be - fore my time, _ but I've _ _ been told _ he nev - er come back from Cop - per - head Road. _

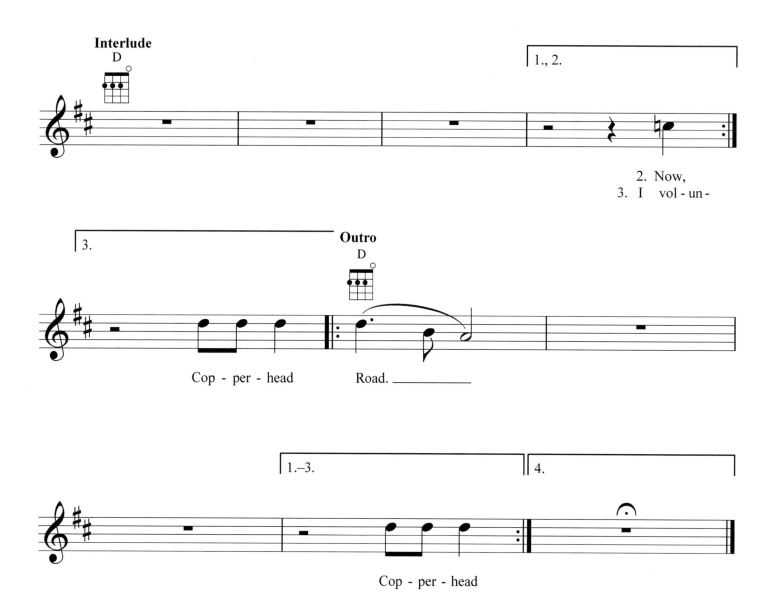

Additional Lyrics

2. Now, Daddy ran the whiskey in a big-block Dodge.
   Bought it at an auction at the Mason's Lodge.
   "Johnson County Sheriff" painted on the side.
   Just shot a coat of primer, then he looked inside.
   Well, him and my uncle tore that engine down.
   I still remember that rumblin' sound.
   Then the sheriff came around in the middle of the night.
   I heard Mama cryin'; knew somethin' wasn't right.
   He was headed down to Knoxville with the weekly load.
   You could smell the whiskey burnin' down Copperhead Road.

3. I volunteered for the Army on my birthday.
   They draft the white trash first 'round here anyway.
   I done two tours of duty in Vietnam.
   I came home with a brand-new plan.
   I'd take the seed from Colombia and Mexico.
   I'd just plant it up a holler down Copperhead Road.
   Now the DEA's got a chopper in the air.
   I wake up screamin' like I'm back over there.
   I learned a thing or two from Charlie, don't you know.
   You better stay away from Copperhead Road.

Achy Breaky Heart
(Don't Tell My Heart)
Words and Music by Don Von Tress

You can tell my feet to hit the floor. Or
self al - read - y knows I'm not o - kay. Or

you can tell my lips to tell my fin - ger - tips they
you can tell my eyes to watch out for my mind. It

won't be reach - ing out for you no more. ___
might be walk - ing out on me to - day. ___ But

Chorus

(1., D.S.) Don't tell my heart, ⟩ my ach - y break - y heart. ___ I
(2.) don't tell my heart, ⟩

just don't think he'd un - der - stand. And

if you tell my heart, my ach - y break - y heart, ___ he

To Coda

might   blow ___ up   and   kill   this   man.   Ooh. _____

1.

2.   *D.S. al Coda*

Coda   **Outro-Chorus**

man.   Don't tell my heart,   my   ach - y break - y heart. ___   I

just   don't think he'd un - der - stand.   And   if   you tell my heart,   my

ach - y break - y heart, ___   he   might blow ___ up   and   kill   this

man.   Ooh. _____

Deep in the Heart of Texas

Words by June Hershey
Music by Don Swander

The sage in bloom is
The cow - boys cry, "Ki -

like per - fume,
yip - pee - yi,"

deep in the
deep in the

A7

heart of Tex - as. _____
heart of Tex - as. _____

Re -
The

minds me of
do - gies bawl,

the one I
and bawl I and

love,
bawl,

deep in the heart of
deep in the heart of

1.
D

A7

2.
D

Tex - as. _____

The

Tex - as. _____

Dream Baby
(How Long Must I Dream)

Words and Music by Cindy Walker

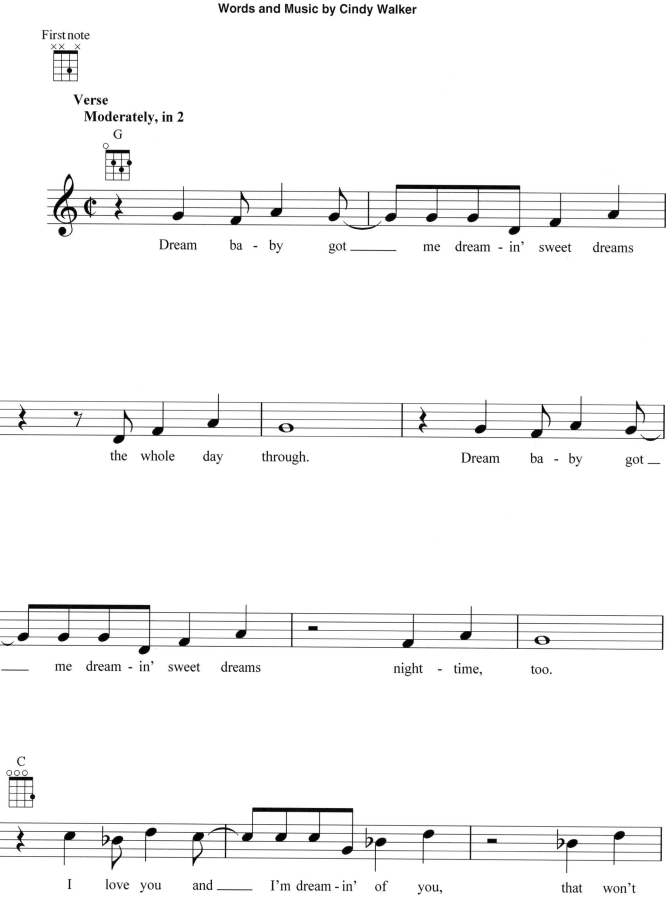

do. _____ Dream ba - by, make ___ me stop my dream - in';

Chorus

you can make my dreams _ come true. Sweet

dream ba - by. Sweet

dream ba - by. Sweet

dream ba - by. How

long must I dream? _____

Eleanor Rigby

Words and Music by John Lennon and Paul McCartney

Additional Lyrics

2. Father McKenzie writing the words of a sermon that no one will hear,
No one comes near.
Look at him working, darning his socks in the night when there's nobody there,
What does he care?

3. Eleanor Rigby died in the church and was buried along with her name,
Nobody came.
Father McKenzie wiping the dirt from his hands as he walks from the grave,
No one was saved.

Fallin'

Words and Music by Alicia Keys

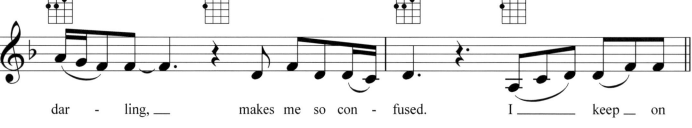

Chorus

fall - in' in and out ___ of love with - a you. I ___

nev - er loved some - one ___ the way that I love-a you, oh, oh.

Verse

2. I ___ nev-er felt this-a way. ___ How do you give me so much

pleas - ure and cause me so much pain? ___ Yeah, ___ yeah. ___ Just when I

think ___ I'm tak-ing more than would a fool, ___ I ___ start

fall - in' ___ back in love with you. ___ I ___ keep ___ on

Chorus

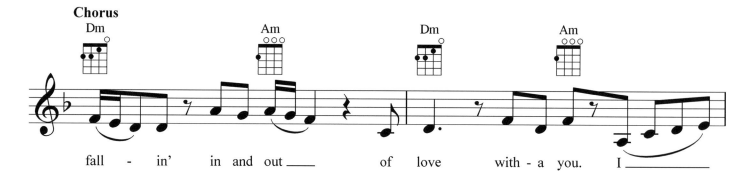

fall - in' in and out ____ of love with - a you. I ____

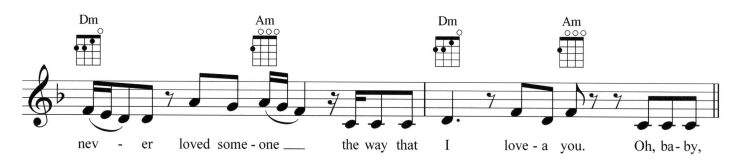

nev - er loved some - one ____ the way that I love - a you. Oh, ba - by,

Bridge

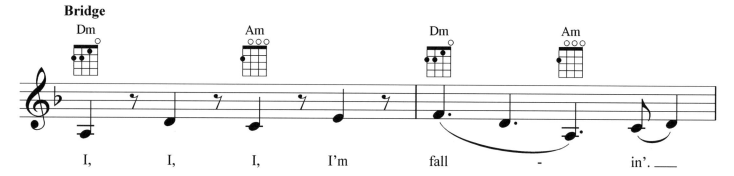

I, I, I, I'm fall - in'. ____

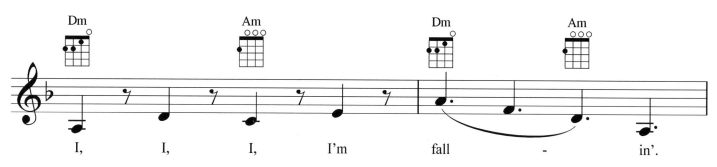

I, I, I, I'm fall - in'. ____

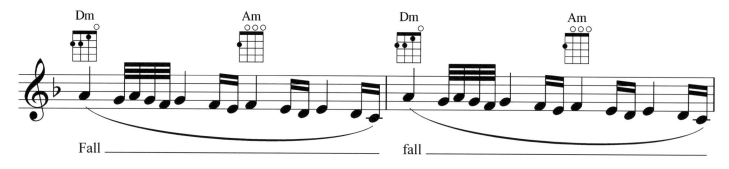

Fall ____ fall ____

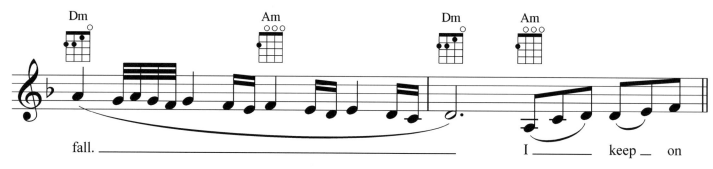

fall. ____ I ____ keep ___ on

24

Hey Liley, Liley Lo
(Married Man Gonna Keep Your Secret)

Words and Music by Elizabeth Austin and Alan Lomax
Additional Words and Music by Alan Lomax

ha - ma moon is shin - in' bright, hey li - ley,
wom - an talk - in' to her man, hey li - ley,
Sun gone down and the moon's on fi - ah, hey li - ley,

li - ley lo. _____ Histe your win - dow, raise it high - er,
li - ley lo. _____ Talk - in' sweet and soft and low,
li - ley lo. _____ Pa - pa's gone and Ma - ma's sleep - in',

hey li - ley, li - ley lo. _____ Sun done set the
hey li - ley, li - ley lo. _____ Come on, ba - by, it's
hey li - ley, li - ley lo. _____ Dark out here, no -

1., 2.

moon on fi - ah, hey li - ley, li - ley lo. _____
time to go, hey li - ley, li - ley lo. _____
bod - y peep - in', hey li - ley,

Coda

3.   D.C. al Coda   Verse

li - ley lo. _____   4. My heart will keep your se - cret,

27

Verses from the original song:

Married man gonna keep your secret,
Hey liley, liley lo.
Married man gonna keep your secret,
Hey liley, liley lo.

Single boy gonna talk about you,
Hey liley, liley lo.
Single boy gonna talk about you,
Hey liley, liley lo.

Day-O
(The Banana Boat Song)

Words and Music by Irving Burgie and William Attaway

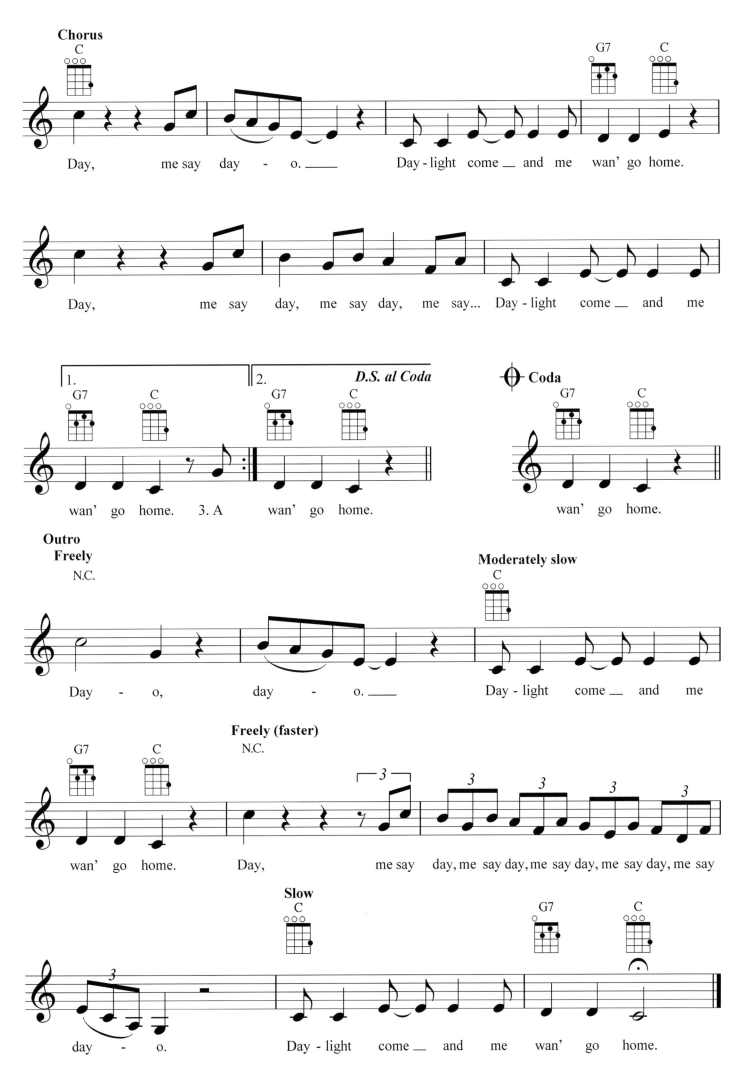

The Hokey Pokey

Words and Music by Charles P. Macak, Tafft Baker and Larry LaPrise

First note

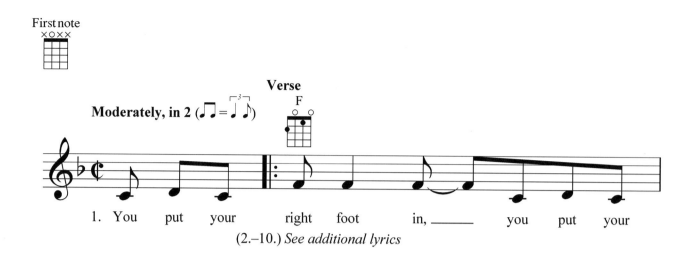

Verse

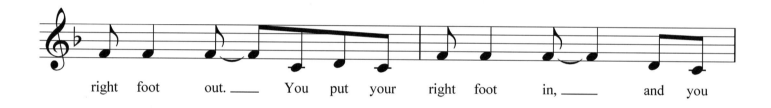

1. You put your right foot in, _____ you put your

(2.–10.) *See additional lyrics*

right foot out. _____ You put your right foot in, _____ and you

shake it all a - bout. You do the Hok - ey Pok - ey, and you

turn your - self a - round. That's what it's all a -

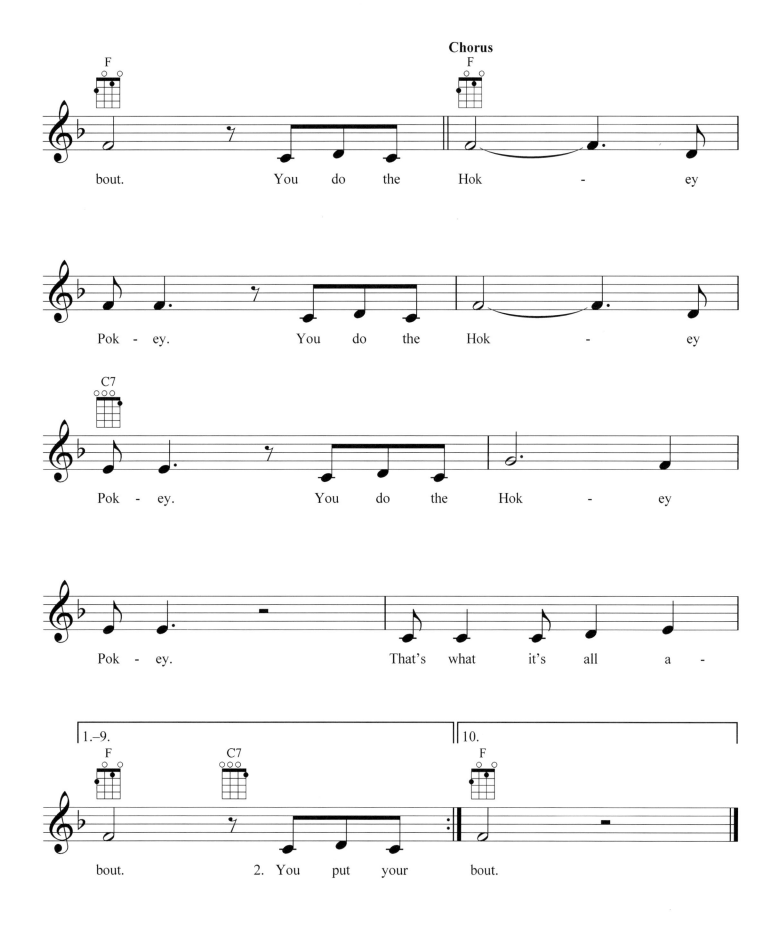

Additional Lyrics

2nd time: left foot
3rd time: right arm
4th time: left arm
5th time: right elbow
6th time: left elbow

7th time: head
8th time: right hip
9th time: left hip
10th time: whole self

I Need to Know

Words and Music by Cory Rooney and Marc Anthony

Iko Iko

Words and Music by Rosa Lee Hawkins, Barbara Ann Hawkins, Joan Marie Johnson, Joe Jones, Maralyn Jones, Sharon Jones and Jessie Thomas

First note

1. My grand-ma and your grand-ma were sit-ting by the fire.

My grand-ma says to your grand-ma, "I'm gon-na set your flag on fire." Talk-in' 'bout

Chorus

hey now! Hey now! I-ko, I-ko, un-day.

Jock-a-mo fee-no ai na-né. Jock-a-mo fee na-né.

Verse

2. Look at my king all dressed in red.
3. My flag boy and your flag boy
4. See that man all dressed in green?

It's Your Thing

Words and Music by Rudolph Isley, Ronald Isley and O'Kelly Isley

First note

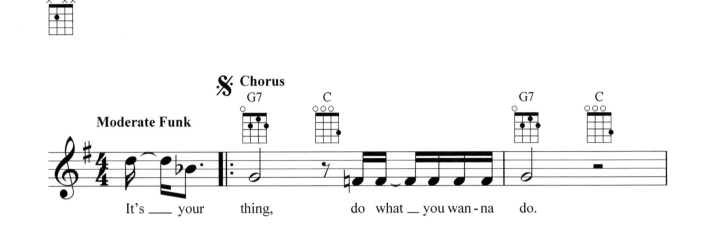

Jambalaya
(On the Bayou)

Words and Music by Hank Williams

The Name Game

Words and Music by Lincoln Chase and Shirley Elliston

The first   let - ter of the name,   I treat it   like it was - n't there.

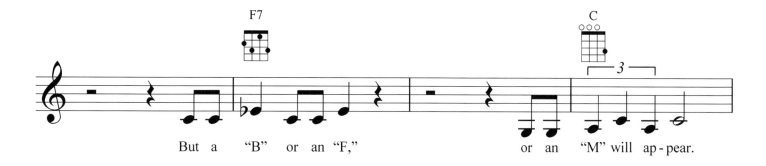

F7   C

But a   "B"   or an "F,"   or an   "M" will ap - pear.

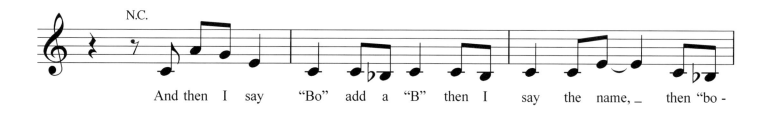

N.C.

And then I   say   "Bo" add a "B" then I   say   the   name,   then "bo -

F7

na - na fan - na" and   "fo."   And then I   say the name a - gain   with an

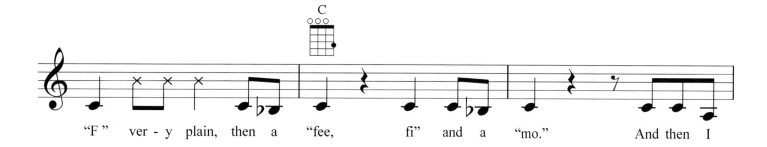

C

"F"   ver - y plain, then a   "fee,   fi"   and a   "mo."   And then I

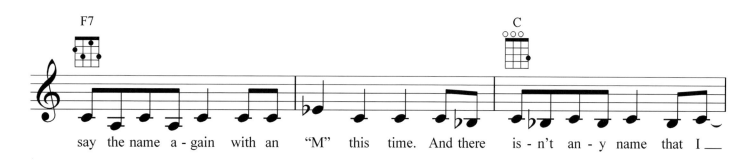

F7   C

say the name a - gain   with an   "M" this   time. And there   is - n't an - y name that I ___

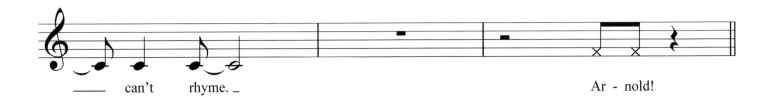

can't rhyme. _   Ar - nold!

Chorus

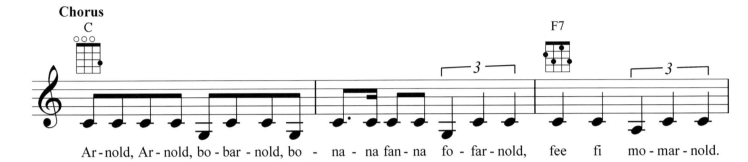

Ar - nold, Ar - nold, bo - bar - nold, bo - na - na fan - na fo - far - nold,   fee   fi   mo - mar - nold.

Bridge

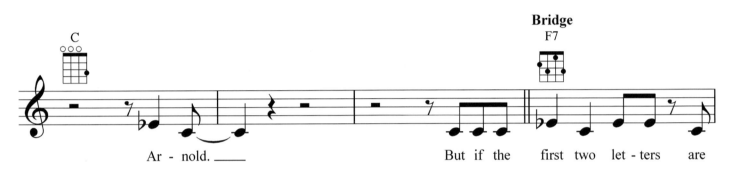

Ar - nold. _____   But if the   first two   let - ters   are

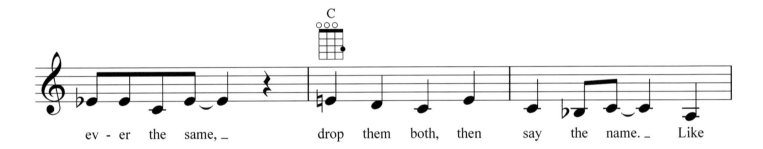

ev - er the same, _   drop them both, then   say   the name. _   Like

Bob,   Bob, drop the "B's," Bo - ob.   Or   Fred,   Fred, drop the "F's." Fo - red.   Or

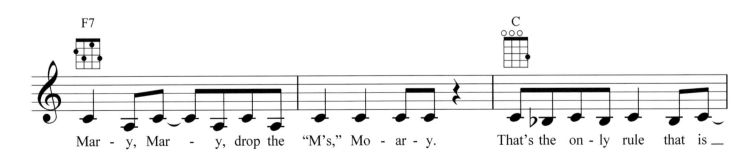

Mar - y, Mar - y, drop the "M's," Mo - ar - y.   That's the on - ly rule that is _

Okie from Muskogee

Words and Music by Merle Haggard and Roy Edward Burris

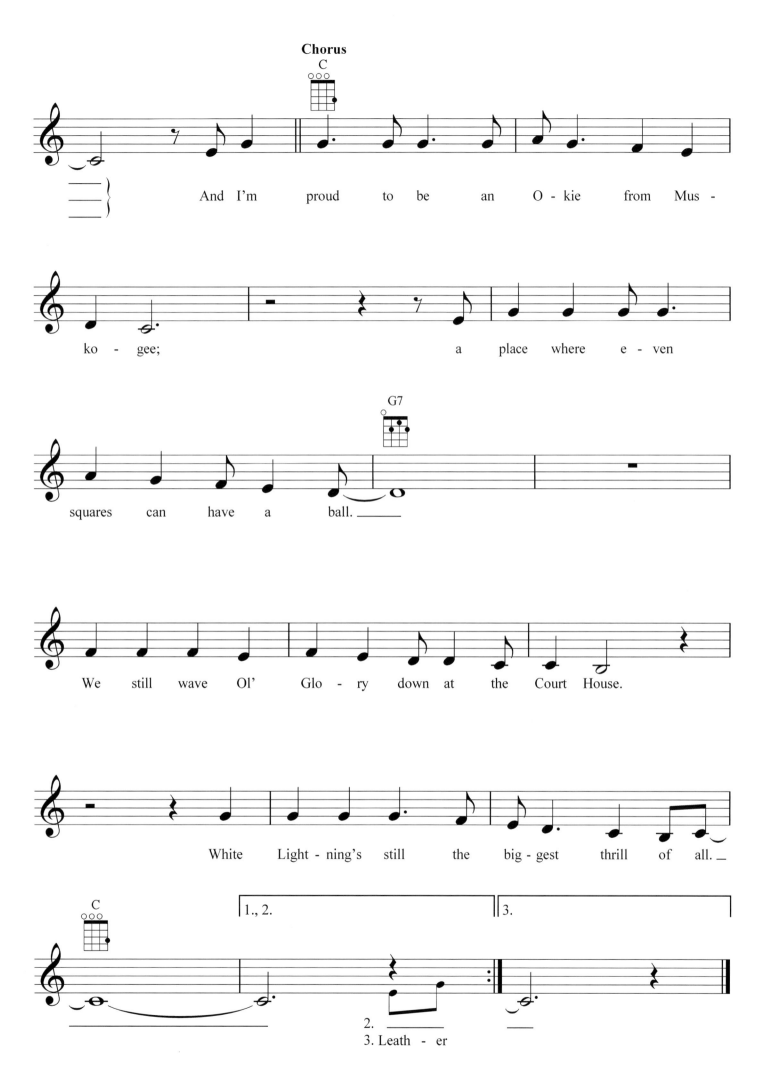

Chorus

And I'm proud to be an O - kie from Mus - ko - gee; a place where e - ven squares can have a ball. _____ We still wave Ol' Glo - ry down at the Court House. White Light - ning's still the big - gest thrill of all. ___

1., 2.

3.

2. _____

3. Leath - er

Oye Como Va

Words and Music by Tito Puente

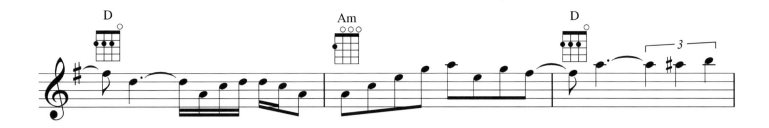

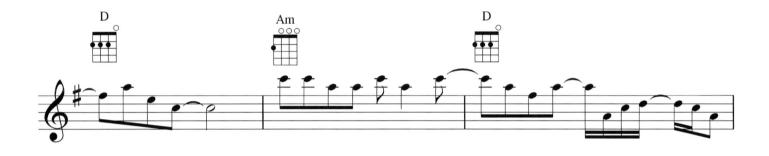

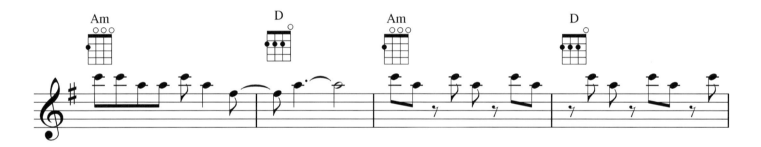

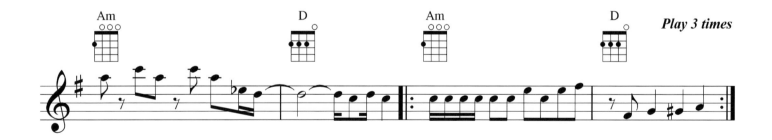

Outro

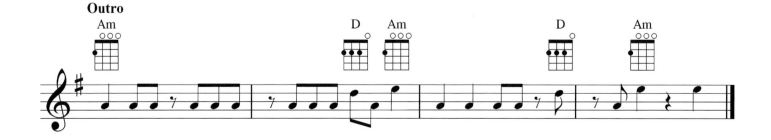

Pistol Packin' Mama

Words and Music by Al Dexter

First note

Verse
Bright Country, in 2

F

1. Drink - in' beer in a cab - a - ret _____ and
2. She kicked out my wind - shield, _____ she
3.–6. *See additional lyrics*

C7

was I hav - in' fun! Un - til one night she
hit me o - ver the head. She cussed and cried and

F

caught me right, _____ and now I'm on the run. }
said I'd lied, _____ and wished that I was dead. }

Chorus

F

Lay that pis - tol down, babe, lay that pis - tol

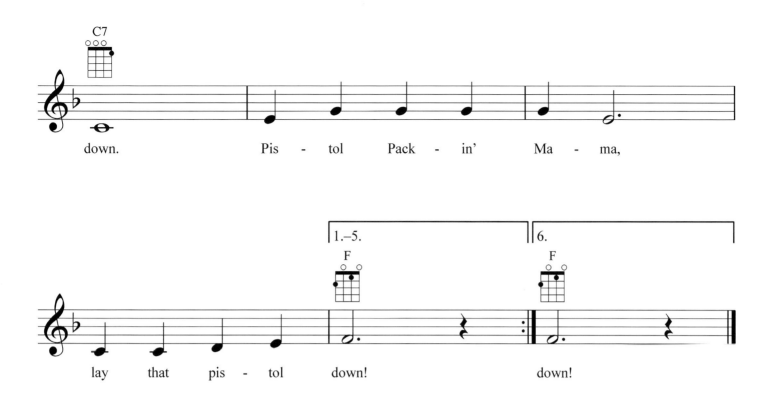

down.   Pis - tol   Pack - in'   Ma - ma,

lay   that   pis - tol   down!   down!

Additional Lyrics

3. Drinkin' beer in a cabaret
   And dancing with a blonde,
   Until one night she shot out the light.
   Bang! That blonde was gone.

4. I'll see you ev'ry night, babe,
   I'll woo you ev'ry day.
   I'll be your regular daddy
   If you'll put that gun away.

5. Drinkin' beer in a cabaret
   And was havin' fun,
   Until one night she caught me right,
   And now I'm on the run.

6. Now there was old Al Dexter,
   He always had his fun.
   But with some lead, she shot him dead.
   His honkin' days were done.

That's the Way
(I Like It)

Words and Music by Harry Wayne Casey and Richard Finch

Do do ___ do ___ do do do do do ___ do. ___

Do do ___ do ___ do do do do do ___ do. ___

𝄋 Chorus

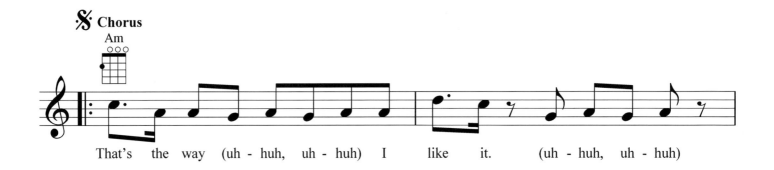

That's the way (uh - huh, uh - huh) I like it. (uh - huh, uh - huh)

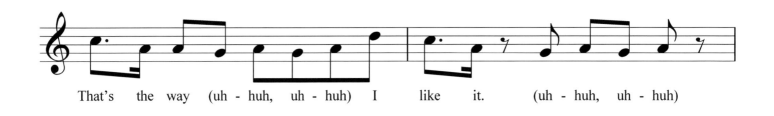

That's the way (uh - huh, uh - huh) I like it. (uh - huh, uh - huh)

To Coda ⊕

That's the way (uh - huh, uh - huh) I like it. (uh - huh, uh - huh)

That's the way (uh - huh, uh - huh) I like it. (uh - huh, uh - huh)

Verse
Dm7

1. When you take me ____ by the hand, _ tell me I'm ____ your lov - in'
2. When I get to ____ be in your arms, _ when we're all, ____ all a -

man, when you give __ me __ all your love and
lone, when you whis - per ____ sweet in my ear,

1. do it, babe, _ the ver - y best you can, oh.
2. when you turn, _ turn me

D.S. al Coda

on, oh.

Bridge
Dm7

⊕ **Coda**

Say ____ o - kay. (uh-huh) That's the way. (uh-huh) That's the way. (uh - huh)

A Horse with No Name

Words and Music by Dewey Bunnell

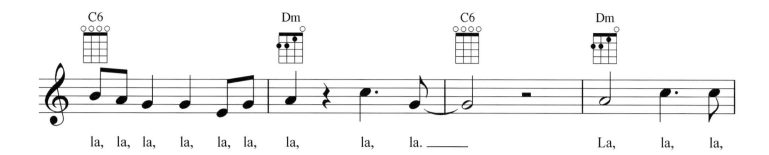

la, la, la, la, la, la, la, la, la. _____ La, la, la,

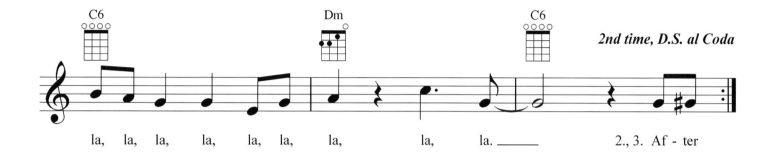

2nd time, D.S. al Coda

la, la, la, la, la, la, la, la, la. _____ 2., 3. Af - ter

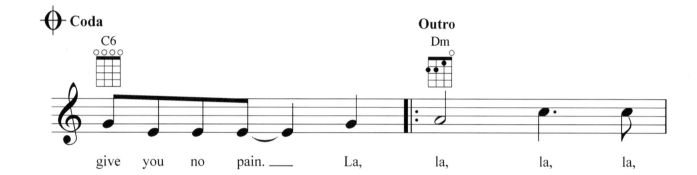

Coda

Outro

give you no pain. __ La, la, la, la,

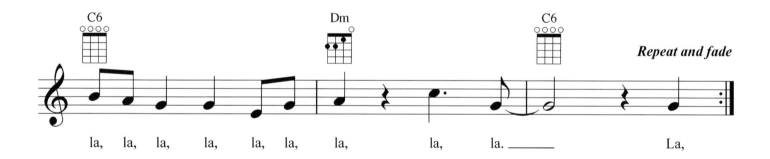

Repeat and fade

la, la, la, la, la, la, la, la, la. _____ La,

Additional Lyrics

2. After two days in the desert sun, my skin began to turn red.
   After three days in the desert fun, I was looking at a river bed.
   And the story it told of a river that flowed made me sad to think it was dead.
   (Skip to Chorus)

3. After nine days, I let the horse run free 'cause the desert had turned to sea.
   There were plants and birds and rocks and things, there were sand and hills and rings.
   The ocean is a desert with its life underground and the perfect disguise above.
   Under the cities lies a heart made of ground, but the humans will give no love.

Tulsa Time

Words and Music by Danny Flowers

goin' to show them all ____ this time. ____ 'Cause you
real - ly had a flash ___ this time. ____ And I

know I ain't no fool - in', I don't need no more school - in'. I was
had no bus' - ness leav - in' and no - bod - y would be griev - in' if I

Chorus

born to just ___ walk ___ the line. ____ Liv - in' on Tul - sa time, __
went on back to Tul - sa time. ____ Liv - in' on Tul - sa time, __

____ liv - in' on Tul - sa time. ____ Well, you
____ liv - in' on Tul - sa time. ____ Gon - na

know I been through it when I set my watch back to it,
set my back to it, 'cause you know I've been through it,

1.
liv - in' on ___ Tul - sa time. ____

2.
2. Well, ____

Use Me

Words and Music by Bill Withers

Waltz Across Texas

Words and Music by Talmadge Tubb

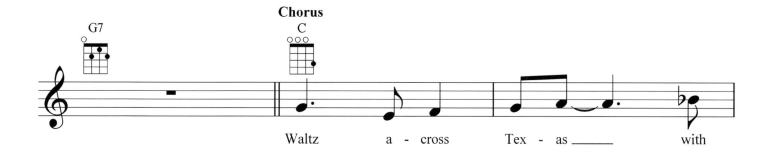

Chorus

Waltz a - cross Tex - as _____ with

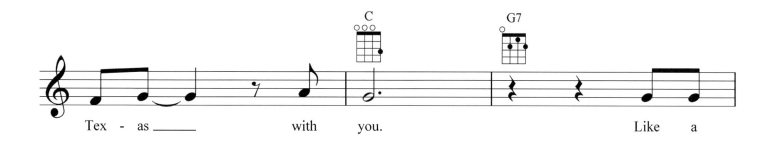

you in my arms, waltz a - cross

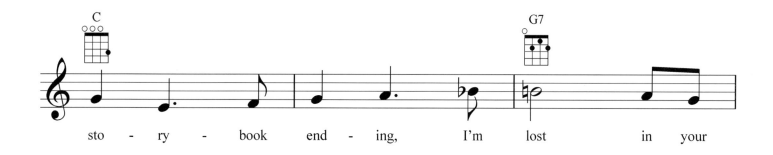

Tex - as _____ with you. Like a

sto - ry - book end - ing, I'm lost in your

charms, and I could waltz a - cross Tex - as _____ with

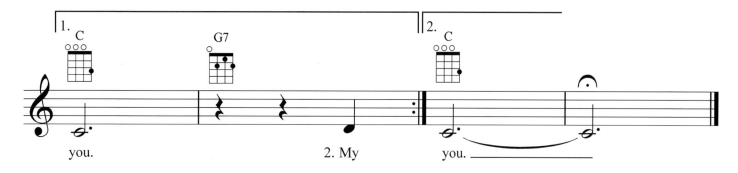

you. 2. My you. _____

UKULELE CHORD SONGBOOKS

This series features convenient 6" x 9" books with complete lyrics and chord symbols for dozens of great songs. Each song also includes chord grids at the top of every page and the first notes of the melody for easy reference.

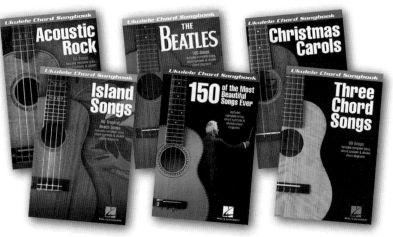

ACOUSTIC ROCK

60 tunes: American Pie • Band on the Run • Catch the Wind • Daydream • Every Rose Has Its Thorn • Hallelujah • Iris • More Than Words • Patience • The Sound of Silence • Space Oddity • Sweet Talkin' Woman • Wake up Little Susie • Who'll Stop the Rain • and more.
00702482 . . . . $15.99

THE BEATLES

100 favorites: Across the Universe • Carry That Weight • Dear Prudence • Good Day Sunshine • Here Comes the Sun • If I Fell • Love Me Do • Michelle • Ob-La-Di, Ob-La-Da • Revolution • Something • Ticket to Ride • We Can Work It Out • and many more.
00703065 . . . . $19.99

BEST SONGS EVER

70 songs: All I Ask of You • Bewitched • Edelweiss • Just the Way You Are • Let It Be • Memory • Moon River • Over the Rainbow • Someone to Watch over Me • Unchained Melody • You Are the Sunshine of My Life • You Raise Me Up • and more.
00117050 . . . . $16.99

CHILDREN'S SONGS

80 classics: Alphabet Song • "C" Is for Cookie • Do-Re-Mi • I'm Popeye the Sailor Man • Mickey Mouse March • Oh! Susanna • Polly Wolly Doodle • Puff the Magic Dragon • The Rainbow Connection • Sing • Three Little Fishies (Itty Bitty Poo) • and many more.
00702473 . . . . $17.99

CHRISTMAS CAROLS

75 favorites: Away in a Manger • Coventry Carol • The First Noel • Good King Wenceslas • Hark! the Herald Angels Sing • I Saw Three Ships • Joy to the World • O Little Town of Bethlehem • Still, Still, Still • Up on the Housetop • What Child Is This? • and more.
00702474 . . . . $14.99

CHRISTMAS SONGS

55 Christmas classics: Do They Know It's Christmas? • Frosty the Snow Man • Happy Xmas (War Is Over) • Jingle-Bell Rock • Little Saint Nick • The Most Wonderful Time of the Year • White Christmas • and more.
00101776 . . . . $14.99

ISLAND SONGS

60 beach party tunes: Blue Hawaii • Day-O (The Banana Boat Song) • Don't Worry, Be Happy • Island Girl • Kokomo • Lovely Hula Girl • Mele Kalikimaka • Red, Red Wine • Surfer Girl • Tiny Bubbles • Ukulele Lady • and many more.
00702471 . . . . $16.99

150 OF THE MOST BEAUTIFUL SONGS EVER

150 melodies: Always • Bewitched • Candle in the Wind • Endless Love • In the Still of the Night • Just the Way You Are • Memory • The Nearness of You • People • The Rainbow Connection • Smile • Unchained Melody • What a Wonderful World • Yesterday • and more.
00117051 . . . . $24.99

PETER, PAUL & MARY

Over 40 songs: And When I Die • Blowin' in the Wind • Goodnight, Irene • If I Had a Hammer (The Hammer Song) • Leaving on a Jet Plane • Puff the Magic Dragon • This Land Is Your Land • We Shall Overcome • Where Have All the Flowers Gone? • and more.
00121822 . . . . $14.99

THREE CHORD SONGS

60 songs: Bad Case of Loving You • Bang a Gong (Get It On) • Blue Suede Shoes • Cecilia • Get Back • Hound Dog • Kiss • Me and Bobby McGee • Not Fade Away • Rock This Town • Sweet Home Chicago • Twist and Shout • You Are My Sunshine • and more.
00702483 . . . . $15.99

TOP HITS

31 hits: The A Team • Born This Way • Forget You • Ho Hey • Jar of Hearts • Little Talks • Need You Now • Rolling in the Deep • Teenage Dream • Titanium • We Are Never Ever Getting Back Together • and more.
00115929 . . . . $14.99

Prices, contents, and availability subject to change without notice.

www.halleonard.com